# THE DOORS AND GATES OF
# CHARLESTON

# THE DOORS AND GATES OF
# CHARLESTON

JOSEPH F. THOMPSON

*For Lollie
From Jean*

UNIVERSITY OF
SOUTH CAROLINA PRESS

Published in Columbia, South Carolina, by the
University of South Carolina Press

Printed in Hong Kong by Everbest Printing Co., Ltd. through Four Colour Imports, Ltd.

Thompson, Joseph F., 1931–
    The doors and gates of Charleston / Joseph F. Thompson.
        p.    cm.
    Includes bibliographical references and index.
    ISBN 0-87249-745-3
    1. Doors—South Carolina—Charleston. 2. Gates—South Carolina—
Charleston. I. Title
NA3010. T46 1990
721' .822' 09757915—dc20                          90-40814

*Dedicated to those
visionaries past and
present who have
saved Charleston for
the world to share.*

## ACKNOWLEDGMENTS

I wish to thank the following individuals for their encouragement, help and support:

Herbert DeCosta for pointing me in the right direction.

My good friend Robert Isbell, for lending his writing skills to improve the text of the book.

Jan Karon, for crystallizing the focus of the book early on and helping me with the original copy.

Charlene Swansea, Charles "Pete" Wyrick, Sandra Hermann, Henry Cauthin and Beth Moore.

Special thanks to everyone at City Graphics.

# CONTENTS

# THE DOORS AND GATES OF
# CHARLESTON

# PREFACE

Azaleas come to bloom on the peninsula long before crocuses appear in the far upcountry, and in these first tender days of spring the old city's aristocratic ghost spreads over the land.

It is then that ancient secrets are shared. No other antiquity transports a visitor with such clarity as does Charleston in the spring. Its flowered warmth is insistent of a still-lived past, and the dark, moist earth of its gardens promises everlasting renewal.

As visitors stroll the lanes called Longitude and Ropemakers, the alleys called Zig Zag and St. Michaels, their senses are regaled by peoples past: shopkeepers, tinkers, carpenters, ironmongers and gardeners. There is no need for hurried dosings of colonial history to recall the past. In the spring, the past comes home. It carries you back in gentle harbor winds that tell of old Barbadian ties; it delights you in cloistered gardens with scents of gardenias, wild roses and jasmine. And from its great homes with their high porticos, it speaks for merchants of the sea, and for planters and overlords of a young nation's beginnings.

In every part of the old city, the homes are unmistakably Charleston. Their architecture dates for the most part from England's Georgian era. But it was practical use that governed their shape and dimensions. There was need to capture the harbor breeze in summer, to harness the southern sun in winter, and to enjoy space and privacy on small but precious plots of a confining peninsula. Therefore, most single- and double-house dwellings are similar. Together they are a mosaic upon which Charleston's singular mark is laid.

Although Charleston gathered cultures from throughout the old world—England, Ireland, Wales, Scotland, France and Germany among them—there is little to suggest eclectic architecture. The first families chose function first; then came beauty. While basics of style were borrowed from London, it was utility more than any other element that sculpted Charleston's magnificent profile.

But as new wealth came and as an independent culture evolved, there was an understandable yen to distinguish one's home in the neighborhood. Therefore, useful adornments were added. Among the most apparent can now be seen in the woodcrafting of handsome doors, and in the ironwork of grilles and fences and gateways.

It is to this subtle difference among Charleston's treasures that this book pays tribute. The polished doors and the finely wrought gates tell a story of individual tastes that entwine lovingly through the whole of the city.

# PRE-REVOLUTIONARY
## 1720–1783

The middle decades of the Eighteenth Century were times of growth and great consequence for Charleston. They were marked by distinctive homes with their handsome moldings, fanlights and doorways that showed Georgian influences. And, as a common complement, there were striking ironworks.

But the iron gates and fences were designed for more than beauty. They made an artful camouflage, half revealing, half concealing secluded gardens and arcaded basements that raised houses above flood level, and elevated upper drawing rooms to take advantage of cool sea breezes.

Gates and fences existed before 1740, but many were destroyed in the fires of 1778. Then some were melted down to make armaments during the American Revolution.

The early wrought iron of Charleston was of British origin. It emulated the patterns and styles seen in England during the first seventy-five years of the Eighteenth Century. There were French styles, too, but none had lasting or profound influence in the city.

The designs and techniques were rich but simple. Cheerful colors—bright hues of blue and green, set off with metallic—enhanced many of the gates and fences. They were a sharp contrast to the black ironwork of Charleston today.

LUNETTE
(IN THE PLANE OF A WALL) an area
enframed by an arch or vault.

And, as concessions to the hot summers, wrought-iron balconies abounded, and later great galleries or piazzas were attached to the southern walls of buildings. These complemented balustrades and passageway lunettes, along with window grilles, which are beautifully typified at 54 Broad. Here the grilles are wrought-iron scrolls and bars, embellished with cast-iron buds and flowers.

It was in 1772 that a minor event left a lasting visual effect upon the city. The parishioners of St. Michael's imported from England a communion railing—a piece of simple elegance befitting their stately church at Meeting and Broad Streets. It was from this modest example that Charleston's ironworkers, no match for their fancy European counterparts, began vigorous production based upon the railing's simplicity. Incapable of crafting fancy florid leaves, vines, berries and heraldic devices, the local smiths found expression in the small railing. Throughout the city, variations of the pattern began to appear—the portal gates of St. Philip's Church, for instance, and the balconies of the Henry Middleton house on South Battery.

Best known among the ironworkers of the period were Tunis Tebout and William Johnson. Working independently and as partners, they advertised in newspapers and did work for the Continental Army.

As can be seen in the Miles Brewton House on King Street and the John Edwards home on Meeting Street, architectural styles differed from the heavy designs of later Classic Revival homes. This lighter, more delicate architecture was inspired by the great Scottish architect Robert Adam.

But unlike Robert Adam, most architects of the time were not particularly artful. They were essentially builders who were influenced by the long-established traditions of their craft. The most prominent were trained in Europe: Peter and John Adam Horlbeck, who built the entire building at 54 Broad from materials left over from the Exchange Building; and Ezra Waite from London, who designed the Miles Brewton House, and Samuel Cardy, designer of St. Michael's Church.

Nothing truly authentic remains of the very earliest buildings. Yet, seventy-three pre-revolutionary houses, all of the Colonial style, still can be seen. But many of the doors did not survive, and original paneling has been replaced by modern substitutes.

Of the surviving examples, there are two general types:

The *single house*, which is one room wide and standing sideways to the street. Its entrance leads to the portico rather than directly into the house. Widely evident in Charleston, excellent examples may be seen at the Robert Pringle House on Tradd Street and the Robert Brewton House on Church Street.

The *double house,* two rooms wide and basically square, has its doorway directly off the street. The Horry House on Meeting Street exemplifies the style, but the Miles Brewton House is probably the archetype.

Architectural influences were chiefly English, softened with a blend of Dutch and French, although nothing undeniably Gallic is in evidence to suggest a French influence of any consequence.

In the six years prior to the Revolutionary War, houses were built with larger dimension and greater richness than in previous times. Most were inventive demonstrations of English-Georgian architecture. They had begun to reflect the expression and vitality of people on the threshold of independence.

PRE-REVOLUTIONARY

| | |
|---|---|
| 1. 19 Archdale | 7. 69 Church | 17. 36 Meeting |
| 2. 106 Broad St. | 8. 71 Church | 18. 37 Meeting |
| 3. 110 Broad St. | 9. 87 Church | 19. 59 Meeting |
| 4. 17 Chalmers | 10. 94 Church | 20. 80 Meeting |
| 5. 39 Church | 11. 95 East Bay | 21. 20 Montague |
| 6. 59 Church | 12. 99-101 East Bay | 22. 32 South Battery |
| | 13. 27 King | 23. 54 Tradd |
| | 14. 15 Meeting | 24. 70 Tradd |
| | 15. 30 Meeting | 25. 106 Tradd |
| | 16. 34 Meeting | 26. 126 Tradd |

*Detail of door knocker.*

**19 Archdale Street.**
*Philip Porcher House.*
*c. 1765.*

**106 Broad Street.**
*Dr. John Lining House.*
*1715.*

**110 Broad Street.**
*William Harvey House.*
*1728.*
*Purchased in 1756*
*by Ralph Izard.*
*Once the residence of*
*Joel Roberts Poinsett,*
*who brought the*
*poinsettia to*
*America.*

*Detail of door knocker.*

### 17 Chalmers Street.
*The Pink House. c. 1712.*
*Believed to have been a tavern in the Colonial period.*
*Walls are of West Indian coral stone.*
*Note antiquated tile roof.*

**39 Church Street.**
*George Eveleigh House. 1743. Gate is example of locally characteristic strap wrought iron, formed in "S" scroll ornaments. Lattice of flat straps at bottom. Indicative of transitional period from wrought iron to cast iron.*

*Detail of doorbell on gate column.*

*Georgian architecture. Garden contains one of the city's largest magnolia trees.*

**59 Church Street**
*Thomas Rose House. 1735.*
*Piazzas and gateway added*
*during the restoration of the*
*house in 1929.*

**69 Church Street.**
*Jacob Motte House. 1745.
Wrought iron added later.
Piazzas on the south side of the
house were removed in 1960
and the front door was restored
on the street side.*

**71 Church Street.**
*Colonel Robert Brewton House. c. <u>1720.</u>
Believed to be the earliest example of the "single
house," i.e., one room wide, end of house to the
sidewalk, porches to the south or west and
north walls windowless.*

That is 278 years ago.

*Detail of fanlight.*

**87 Church Street.**
*Heyward-Washington House.*
*1772. Built by a wealthy rice*
*planter, Daniel Heyward.*

*Detail of door knocker.*

**94 Church Street.**
*Thomas Bee House. c. 1730.*
*Governor Joseph Alston and*
*wife, Theodosia Burr (daughter*
*of Aaron Burr) owned this site.*
*Door is street entrance to*
*piazza, which was added in the*
*early 19th century.*

**95 East Bay Street.**
*c. 1740–1760.*
*English and Dutch architecture.*
*Note pastel-colored exterior.*
*Typical "rainbow row" house.*

**99-101 East Bay Street.**
*Colonel Othniel Beale House.*
*c. 1723–1740. Typical Charleston gate*
*with "S" scrolls in wrought iron straps.*

**27 King Street.**
*Miles Brewton House. c. 1769.*
*One of the finest examples of Georgian*
*architecture in America. Designed by Ezra*
*Waite. Wrought iron gates antedate the*
*Revolutionary War. Molded picket uprights,*
*similar to many 18th century London fences.*
*Note large baroque shell at top of overthrow.*

*Example of elliptical door, earliest in Colonial*
*American architecture.*

**15 Meeting Street.**
*John Edwards House. c. 1770.*

*Note "lyre" design in
center of balustrade. Designed
by Julius Ortmann.*

**30 Meeting Street.**
*Isaac Motte House. 1770.*
*Typical early Georgian style.*

**34 Meeting Street.**
*Daniel Elliott Huger House.*
*c. 1760. Exemplifies the "double house" design. Residence of South Carolina's last royal governor. Three piazzas added after 1900.*

**36 Meeting Street.**
c. <u>1740</u>. Georgian architecture.
<u>Good example of the "single</u>
<u>house.</u>" Original woodwork.

*Detail of door knocker.*

**37 Meeting Street.**
*c. 1766. Gate is combination of "S" and "C" scrolls and flat lattice panel wrought iron. Gate added later.*

*Old Charleston refers to the unusual architecture of the "Double-Breasted House" because of its twin bays. Design is a departure from the usual Charleston architecture.*

**59 Meeting Street.**
*Branford-Horry House. 1751–1767.*
*Example of the "double house."*

**80 Meeting Street.**
*St. Michael's Church. 1752–1761.*

**20 Montague Street.**
*William Moultrie House. 1770–1778.*
*Example of neo-classical doorway.*
*Note Greek Ionic pilaster.*

**32 South Battery Street.**
*Colonel John Ashe House. c. 1782.*

**54 Tradd Street.**
*Postmaster Bacot House. c. 1740.*

*Gate is good example of
wrought iron combination of
"S" scrolls and straight bars.*

**70 Tradd Street.**
*Judge Robert Pringle House. c. 1774.*
*Door is street entrance to piazza.*
*Example of "single house."*

224 years old

**106 Tradd Street.**
*Colonel John Stuart House. c. 1772. House built of black cypress. Note Greek Corinthian pilasters.*

*Detail of Greek Corinthian pilaster.*

*Detail of door knocker.*

*All rooms in this house are perfectly proportioned and considered models by archictects.*

**126 Tradd Street.**
*Dr. Peter Fayssoux House. c. 1732.*

126

# POST-REVOLUTIONARY
## 1783–1812

The British withdrew in 1782, and war-weary Charlestonians turned again to their own ways, to private and familiar patterns. Conditions had caused extreme poverty among many, and the whole economy was strained. Yet, typically, Charlestonians looked forward as they struggled. It was remarkable that from this era came expansiveness, and renaissance.

They imported manufactured articles from all over the world—a diversity of English hardware and woolens, French silk and brandies, Canton china, Madras prints, Spanish and Portuguese wine, and Jamaican rum. On their plantations they raised rice and cotton, but the production of indigo ceased, never to be revived.

During this time little occurred to change the city's architectural profile. When construction activity did return, it tended to be for religious, social and philanthropic institutions. And when home building resumed, the structures were for the most part large-scale and simplified.

These you can see as you walk the historic district. Typical representations of the post-revolutionary style can be viewed both up and down Meeting Street. Here you will find breezy piazzas, often in two and three tiers, extending the length of the houses along western and southern exposures. These not only helped shield the houses from direct sun, but also provided airy retreats during fragrant and humid evenings.

But while most of the period was occupied in grand and simple structures that were nearly devoid of ironwork, Charleston native Gabriel Manigault moved against the tide. Unschooled in formal architecture, he traveled abroad to study. When he returned home an avid proponent of English architecture, he set about to give his city's architectural composition a new elegance and refinement. For his Page 68 → brother he designed the Joseph Manigault House. His masterfully executed City Hall at Meeting and Broad helped influence building in Charleston until the War of 1812. His South Carolina Society Hall on Meeting Street, with its S-scrolls and husks repeated the length of the railing, is one of the finest, most attractive wrought iron pieces in the city. The building—set along a tree-lined street, adjacent to a high brick wall and in the shadow of St. Michael's gleaming white spire— symbolizes Charleston to many thousands who have admired it.

As for the ironsmiths of the period, little is known; except for Gabriel Manigault, their trade might have simply vanished. Of those who did continue, they often left creativity to an architect and simply executed designs that others specified.

POST-REVOLUTIONARY

1. 10 Archdale
2. 51 East Bay
3. 55 East Bay
4. 62 Broad
5. 68 Broad
6. 38 Church
7. 6 Gibbes
8. 14 Legare
9. 8 Meeting

10. 51 Meeting
11. 57 Meeting
12. 68 Meeting
13. 69 Meeting
14. 72 Meeting
15. 76 Meeting
16. 77 Meeting
17. 342 Meeting
18. 350 Meeting

**10 Archdale Street.**
*St. John's Lutheran Church.
1816–1818. Excellent example of
locally characteristic strap wrought
iron gates forming "S" and "C"
scrolls. Designed in 1822
by A.P. Reeves.*

*Details of gates.*

**51 East Bay Street**
*John Fraser House c. 1818.*
*Piazzas and garden wall*
*added in 1836.*

*Note classic columns*
*ascending in order,*
*Doric, Ionic and*
*Corinthian.*

**55 East Bay Street**
*c.1812*

*Detail of door knocker.*

*Detail of fanlight.*

**62 Broad Street.**
*The Confederate Home.*
*c. 1800.*

*Detail of door.*

**68 Broad Street.**
*Daniel Ravenel House. c. 1796.*
*One of the oldest residential*
*properties in the city to remain*
*continuously with the same family.*

**38 Church Street.**
*Leseigneur House. c. 1819.*
*Street entrance leads to piazza.*

**6 Gibbes Street.**
*Parker-Drayton House. c. 1806.*
*Example of lattice panel combined*
*with wrought iron scrolls.*

**14 Legare Street.**
*Simmons-Edwards House. 1800.*
*Built by Francis Simmons.*

**14 Legare Street.**

(top left) George Edwards
Gateway. Combination of
wrought iron and wood. Note
bank of wrought iron hearts in
the center of the gate.

(center) Wrought iron grilles by
George Edwards. Details of grilles
on either side of doorway. Note
George Edwards' initials "G" and
"E" designed into grilles.

(left) Detail of "pineapple" finial
atop gates. Originally ordered
from Italy as a set of live-oak
acorns in marble. Instead, Italian
stonemasons carved pine cones,
a popular design in Mediterranean
countries. Similarity between
the shape of the pine cone and
the pineapple resulted in the
confusion. Gates now popularly
named "Pineapple Gates."

**51 Meeting Street.**
*Nathaniel Russell House. 1808.*
*National historic landmark.*
*Considered one of the finest*
*examples of neo-classic*
*architecture.*

*(right) Detail of balcony ironwork. Front central bay contains the initials of the builder, Nathaniel Russell. The balusters scrolled at the center and extremities are typical of the balconies of the period.*

*(below) Door knocker and fanlight.*

*Nathaniel Russell House Gate. Original ironwork.*

**8 Meeting Street.**
*Ladson House. 1800.*

*Cast iron balcony.*

**57 Meeting Street.**
*First (Scots) Presbyterian Church. 1814. Gates and fence consistent with the large classical porch of the building. Solid, simple design. Bars of the gates are set edge-wise, rather than parallel to the street. Gate design similar to that of St. Paul's Church on Coming Street.*

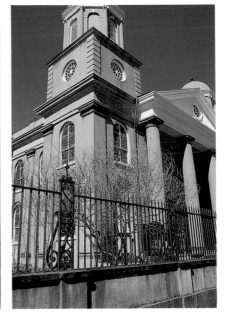

**68 Meeting Street.**
*Prioleau House. 1806.*

*(far left) Detail of Corinthian pilaster cap.*

**69 Meeting Street.**
*Poyas-Mordecai House. 1788.*

63

*Stair rail. Note upright elongated
"S" scrolls, with husks in pairs,
breaking from the scrolls.*

*Detail of lantern standard.
Designed in 1760–70. Lantern
is tin, ornamented with cast
iron rosettes.*

**72 Meeting Street.**
*South Carolina Society Hall.
1804. Designed by Gabriel
Manigault. Portico designed by
Frederick Wesner-1825.*

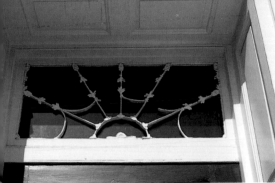

*Detail of fanlight.*

**76 Meeting Street.**
*Elihu Hall House. 1785.*
*Now a church rectory.*

**77 Meeting Street.**
*Court House. 1752-1788. Judge
William Drayton, Architect.
Doorway has been altered
many times.*

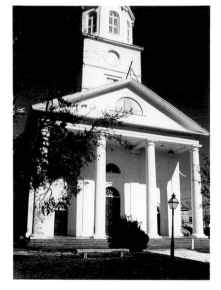

**342 Meeting Street.**
*Second Presbyterian Church.*
*1809-1811. Note damage from*
*Hurricane Hugo, 1989.*

**350 Meeting Street.**
*Joseph Manigault House. 1803.*
*Now owned by the Charleston*
*Museum. Designed by Gabriel*
*Manigault. One of the most*
*perfect Adam style houses in*
*the country.*

*Gatehouse. c. 1790.*

# ANTE-BELLUM
## 1812–1860

As the decade opened, Charleston turned its attention from foreign problems and looked inward to develop its own resources. Incompatible soil and dwindling profits from slavery made cotton less profitable. But despite the burgeoning of industrialism in the rest of the country, Charleston and the South steadfastly clung to the agrarian life.

Thus it seemed an anomaly of the times that the first railroad in the United States began operating on a line between Charleston and the small town of Hamburg, on the South Carolina side of the Savannah River at Augusta. The railroad was a part of the business of agriculture that continued to flourish. Prosperity grew, and by the 1840's it had gained extraordinary proportions. This brought the architect to high favor again, while craftsman and builder diminished in prominence.

For fifty years, lavish and extravagant architecture dominated the Charleston landscape. It was a time of grandiose design that perfected many of the magnificent buildings skirting the Battery like imperious *grande dames* looking out to sea. And of all the distinctive characteristics of the era, one is especially characteristic—the airy, two-story double portico.

During this fertile period of Greek Revival—with its Neo-Greek and Gothic Revival architecture—door surfaces became broader. Details on and around doorways took on a larger scale. Overall, a distinct difference from Georgian design became evident.

Examples of the Greek influence were in the massive Doric columns or pilasters that were applied to public buildings. The lighter, more lyrical Corinthian and Ionic columns were being used for homes. And Robert Mills, Charleston-born and one of America's most esteemed architects, was making his mark upon Charleston and the South. His work included numerous public buildings and residences, the Washington Monument, and America's first fireproof building, at Meeting Street near Chalmers.

In 1826, the College of Charleston engaged a Philadelphia architect named Strickland to plan one of its buildings. Twenty years later the structure was enhanced with a portico and lateral wings designed by amateur architect Colonel E. Brickell White, a Charlestonian. Colonel White, who designed many buildings in the country, went on to develop the spire of St. Philip's Church, which was being rebuilt after the fire of 1835. The St. Philip's spire remains a soaring prominence along Charleston's gentle skyline. Other notable achievements by Colonel White were the Huguenot Church and the Grace Episcopal Church. Also during this period, the firm of Jones & Lee designed the Unitarian Church and St. Luke's Episcopal Church.

Because many ante-bellum dwellings were large, ceilings were high and walls contained tall, narrow windows that extended to the floor. Adjacent balconies were common, and these were protected by cast-iron grilles of

anthemion patterns. The demand for ironwork was considerable, and it was a time
when the best-known ironworkers flourished.

Of these craftsmen, the most prominent
were Germans: J.A.W. Iusti, Christopher
Werner and Frederick Julius Ortmann. Though
they were German by birth, their work was
essentially along English lines.

It was Iusti who fashioned the gates at
St. Michael's, his most notable accomplish-
ment. Today you may see his name in the part
of the gate above the stile.

The very design of the Sword Gates on
Legare Street made Christopher Werner's
work the most well known and memorable.
But impressive as these gates are, the design is
imperfect in that the panels and gates are of
inferior materials; the husks, which break out
from the shafts, are thin and fragile. Werner
came to Charleston from Germany in 1828,
and was known to be working at his trade as
late as 1870. He worked also in copper and
brass, and some of his output can be found on
the grounds of the State House in Columbia.
He crafted the fence at the Elias Vanderhorst
House at Chapel and Alexander Streets, and
probably executed the Hibernian Hall fence
on Meeting Street.

It was Frederick Julius Ortmann whose
influence became widely evident in Charleston.
His pleasing iron designs, the "conventionalized
lyre", are typical and widespread in the ironworks of the city. A notable example of
Ortmann's work is the gates at 34 Broad Street.

The balustrade of the John Edwards home on Meeting Street is another example of a highly developed lyre.

While other interesting architecture continued after the Civil War, the golden era of its antiquity had already been established. From that time until today Charleston has been in a time warp. Except for the ravages of civil conflict, of hurricanes and of a crippling earthquake, the old city has withstood the forces that would change it. Founding families bent with its misfortunes, but what they yielded in prosperity they gained in preservation. For nearly a century Charleston was too poor to rebuild. Its citizens made do with what they had. And what they had was a jewel so precious to be unique in all the world.

Charleston has survived an illustrious past. Even though the periphery of the old city bustles with contemporary commerce, the essence of its old world remains—languid, timeless and beautiful. It is one of America's most beloved places. This in itself might ensure that the glory which you share of it today will likely be in place for your return.

ANTE-BELLUM

1. 1 Broad
2. 1 East Battery
3. 9 East Battery
4. 13 East Battery
5. 21 East Battery
6. 141 East Bay
7. 39 South Battery
8. 61 Church
9. 135 Church
10. 146 Church
11. 66 George
12. 21 King
13. 50 Laurens
14. 32 Legare
15. 1 Meeting
16. 80 Meeting
17. 100 Meeting
18. 105 Meeting

**1 Broad Street.**
*State Bank Building. 1853. Good example of Italianate architecture. Eclectic design not typically Charlestonian.*

*Detail of cast iron door ornament.*

*Detail of ornamental keystone.*

**1 East Battery Street.**
*DeSaussure House. 1850.*
*Wrought iron window balconies*
*probably designed by architect.*
*Example of modified "single house,"*
*with entrance to house on street.*

**9 East Battery Street.**
*Robert William Roper House.*
*c. 1838. Supposedly designed*
*and built by Charlestonian,*
*Colonel Edward Brickell White.*

*Detail of frosted*
*glass door panel.*

*Detail of rope molding*
*around doorway.*

*One of the tallest waterfront houses. Colonnaded portico was destroyed in the earthquake of 1886.*

*Detail of door knocker.*

**13 East Battery Street.**
*William Ravenel House. 1845.*
*Good example of Greek Revival*
*or Neo-Classical.*

**21 East Battery Street.**
*Edmonston-Alston House.*
*Originally built 1817–1825.*
*Refurbished 1838. Grand example*
*of the taste and affluence of 19th*
*Century Charleston.*

**141 East Bay Street.**
*Farmers & Exchange Bank.*
*1853–1859. Example of Moorish*
*eclecticism. Not typically*
*Charlestonian.*

*(below right) Detail of stone*
*pilaster cap.*

*(below) Detail of cast iron*
*door ornament.*

**39 South Battery Street.**
*The Magwood-Moreland
House. 1827. Upper piazza
added later.*

**61 Church Street.**
*First Baptist Church. 1822.*
*Designed by Robert Mills.*

**135 Church Street.**
*Dock Street Theatre. 1835.*
*Rebuilt in 1935. Formerly the*
*Planters Hotel.*

*Note cast iron*
*column ornaments.*

*Wrought iron gate of elongated*
*"S" scrolls and lyre design in*
*center. Lattice work at bottom*
*with cast iron "stars."*

**146 Church Street.**
*St. Philip's Church. 1835.*

*Fans and palmets at top of gate suggest cast iron influence, although they are wrought iron.*

**66 George Street.**
*College of Charleston. Oldest*
*municipal college in America,*
*chartered 1785.*

*(below right) Detail of "S" scroll wrought iron straps of lodge gate.*

*Lodge or gate house built in 1852.*

**66 George Street.**
*College of Charleston.
Central portion of building by
Philadelphia architect Strickland
in 1828. Portico and wings added
by Charleston architect Colonel
E. Brickell White in 1850.*

**21 King Street.**
*Patrick O'Donnell House.*
*c. 1851. Late Italian Renaissance*
*styling. Note heavy decorations*
*above the windows.*

**50 Laurens Street.**
*Gate is a good example of wrought iron "S" scrolls combined with cast iron spearheads and palmets. Wrought iron lattice panel at bottom of gate.*

*Detail of
cast iron "boss".*

**32 Legare Street.**
*The Sword Gates. c. 1848.
Named from the use of swords as
the motif of decoration. Combination of double strap wrought
iron scrolls and cast iron.
Designed by German-born iron
craftsman, Christopher Werner.*

*(above) Details of frosted glass door panel, door knocker and door knobs.*

**1 Meeting Street.**
*John Robertson House. 1846.*

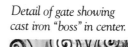

**80 Meeting Street.**
*St. Michael's Church Gate. 1840.*
*Designed by German-born iron*
*craftsman, J.A.W. Iusti. Example*
*of wrought iron combined with*
*cast iron.*

*J.A.W. Iusti's name appears*
*above the gate on stile.*

*Detail of gate showing*
*cast iron "boss" in center.*

*Detail of gate showing*
*chalice and urn design.*

**100 Meeting Street.**
*Fireproof Building. 1822–1828.*

*Gate suggests cast iron
influence, although it is made of
wrought iron straps.*

**105 Meeting Street.**
*Hibernian Hall. 1840.*

*Detail of wrought iron gate overthrow, thought to be designed by Christopher Werner.*

# BIBLIOGRAPHY

Albert Simons and Samuel Lapham, Jr.
*The Early Architecture of Charleston*
1970 — University of South Carolina Press

Alton Deas
*The Early Ironwork of Charleston*
1941 — Bostic & Thornley

Samuel Gaillard Stoney
*This is Charleston*
1944 — Carolina Art Association for Charleston
Civic Services Committee

Arthur Mazyck, Gene Waddell
*Charleston, South Carolina 1883.*
1883 and 1983 — Southern Historical Press

Samuel Gaillard Stoney
*Charleston — Azaleas and Old Bricks*
1937 — Houghton-Mifflin

Jack Leland, William Jordan
*60 Famous Houses of Charleston, South Carolina*
1970-1985 — Charleston News & Courier and
The Evening Post

# INDEX